Adventures in Canadian History

TRAPPED IN THE ARCTIC

Books for Younger Readers by Pierre Berton

The Golden Trail
The Secret World of Og

ADVENTURES IN CANADIAN HISTORY
The Capture of Detroit
The Death of Isaac Brock
Revenge of the Tribes
Canada Under Siege

Bonanza Gold
The Klondike Stampede
Trails of '98
City of Gold

Parry of the Arctic
Jane Franklin's Obsession
Dr. Kane of the Arctic Seas
Trapped in the Arctic

The Railway Pathfinders
The Men in Sheepskin Coats
A Prairie Nightmare
Steel Across the Plains

PIERRE BERTON

Exploring
the Frozen North

TRAPPED IN THE ARCTIC

ILLUSTRATIONS BY PAUL MCCUSKER

M&S

An M&S Paperback Original from
McClelland & Stewart Inc.
The Canadian Publishers

An M&S Paperback Original from McClelland & Stewart Inc.

First printing June 1993

Copyright © 1993 by Pierre Berton Enterprises Ltd.

Canadian Cataloguing in Publication Data

Berton, Pierre, 1920-
Trapped in the Arctic

(Adventures in Canadian history. Exploring the frozen North)
"An M&S paperback original."
Includes index.
ISBN 0-7710-1447-3

1. Arctic regions – Discovery and exploration – English – Juvenile literature.
2. Northwest Passage – Juvenile literature. 3. McClure, Robert, Sir,
1807-1873 – Juvenile literature. 4. Explorers – Canada – Biography –
Juvenile literature. I. Title. II. Series: Berton, Pierre,
1920-   . Adventures in Canadian history. Exploring the frozen North.

G650 1850 B47 1993   j919.804′092   C93-093443-1

Series design by Tania Craan
Cover and text design by Stephen Kenny
Cover illustration by Scott Cameron
Interior illustrations by Paul McCusker
Maps by James Loates
Editor: Peter Carver

Typesetting by M&S

Printed and bound in Canada by Webcom Ltd.

The support of the Government of Ontario through the Ministry of Culture and Communications is acknowledged

McClelland & Stewart Inc.
The Canadian Publishers
481 University Avenue
Toronto, Ontario
M5G 2E9

Contents

Maps appear on pages 26 and 38

The events in this book actually happened as told here. Nothing has been made up. This is a work of non-fiction and there is archival evidence for every story and, indeed, every remark made in this book.

No Way Out

September, 1851. For more than a year, Robert McClure, a British naval officer, cut off entirely from the rest of the world, has been exploring the wriggling channels of the western Arctic, discovering new lands that no white man has ever seen. He has already spent one winter frozen in the ice. Now, as he rounds the northern point of Banks Island, the winter again closes in. Just ahead an apparently safe harbour beckons. He manoeuvres his ship through the ice floes into the sheltering bay. Only later does he realize that he is trapped. There is no way out. He cannot get his vessel back over the shoals that block the entrance. Food is running out. Men are dying of scurvy. Two have gone mad. Will he and his six-dozen men die by inches, here in this friendless land? Are there any other ships in this vast and lonely realm that may come to his aid? He has no way of knowing. He has unlocked the greatest geographical puzzle of the age: the secret of the North West Passage. But can he survive to bask in that glory? A slow and agonizing death stares him in the face. Only a miracle can save him.

Overview

The mysterious Passage

THE GREAT AGE OF EXPLORATION, which captured the imagination of our ancestors, is over – at least on Earth. All the nooks and crannies of our modern world have at last been charted and mapped. We must now reach for the stars.

But there was a time when the earth held many mysteries and some regions were almost as remote as the moon itself – and almost as difficult to reach. Those who were bold enough and ambitious enough to try achieved a fame even greater than that won by the astronauts of our own age.

In Queen Victoria's time (1837–1901), the great celebrities weren't rock stars, movie idols, or sports figures. They were members of that strange and determined breed of explorers prepared to vanish from civilization for years – to cut off all contact with their wives and families, to face disaster, sickness, even death, to seek the source of the Nile or to unlock the secret of the North West Passage.

The Passage! A century and half ago there was magic in that word. Since the days of Columbus, seamen had been seeking a shorter route through North and South America – two continents that acted as a barrier between Europe and the treasures of the Orient.

To us this passion seems very strange. Long before 1850, when our story begins, it was clear that even if a Passage was found, it would be useless. If it existed at all, it was hidden away in the mists of the Arctic – unknown land that had never been mapped or charted.

Yet the *idea* of such a Passage had been so firmly fixed in human minds for some three centuries that it still lured ships and seamen into the frozen world. Men tried to find it, as they sought to reach the summit of Everest – for no practical reason, only because it was there.

It was agreed that whoever found such a Passage would be celebrated beyond reason – he would become an heroic figure, showered with wealth, welcomed into the palaces of princes, honoured above all others. Parliament had offered a reward of ten thousand pounds to anyone who could find the Passage – at least half a million dollars in today's money.

For an ambitious explorer in the mid-nineteenth century, the Passage was the greatest of all prizes. This is the story of an ambitious man – ambitious to a fault – who was the first to discover, not *the* Passage, but *a* Passage. For, as it turned out, there are several lanes of water wriggling between the Arctic islands, connecting the great Atlantic and Pacific oceans.

For the best part of two centuries, British seamen had tried to penetrate the Arctic mystery. If you look at the map of Canada's Arctic, you will see the names of some of these men who explored that vast and forbidding territory – Hudson Bay, Baffin Bay, Davis Strait, Bylot Island – all these commemorate the daring explorers who were the first white men to chart these corners of the frozen world.

Back in the days of Elizabeth I (1558–1603), that old sea dog Martin Frobisher had declared that the discovery of the Passage "is still the only thing left undone, whereby a notable mind might be made famous and remarkable." Frobisher made three voyages between 1576 and 1578 on a vain quest for the elusive channel.

Others followed. In 1585 John Davis rediscovered Greenland, which had been forgotten after the failure of the Norse colonies three centuries before, but he didn't find the Passage.

Henry Hudson sailed through the strait that bears his name in 1610. Bursting into a seemingly limitless sea, he thought he had succeeded in reaching the Pacific. He was wrong. In fact he had discovered Hudson Bay – which would immortalize his name, but only after he met his death at the hands of a mutinous crew.

In 1616 Hudson's pilot, Robert Bylot, and his brilliant sidekick, William Baffin, left their names on two Arctic islands, travelling three hundred miles (480 km) farther north than any white man before them. But they didn't find the Passage.

When Luke Foxe reported in 1631 that there could be no route to the Orient south of the Arctic Circle, he killed all hope of a practical passage. That slowed down the search, but didn't end it.

The Arctic still remained a blank on the map, except for parts of Henry Hudson's vast bay and Bylot and Baffin's great Arctic island.

Two overland explorers managed to reach the Arctic waters. Samuel Hearne arrived at the mouth of the Copper-mine River in 1771, and Alexander Mackenzie reached the delta of the river named for him in 1789. The Arctic itself remained a mystery.

After the end of the Napoleonic Wars in 1815, the search for the Passage began again. One may well ask why. The fact is that, with the world at peace, the Royal Navy had to find work for its officers, ninety percent of whom had nothing to do.

For an ambitious man like Robert McClure, there was little chance for promotion. There were just too many offi-cers. In fact at one point there was one naval officer in Great Britain for every three sailors! Only by performing some impossible and miraculous feat could a man like McClure hope to gain promotion.

And so, with nothing to lose but their lives, and with an over-abundance of sea-going craft anchored in the har-bours, the men of the Royal Navy launched a new age of exploration.

In those days the Canadian North was almost entirely unknown. We know it now from photographs, illustra-tions, films, and travellers' accounts. If we have the fare we can board a plane and fly all the way to the Arctic Ocean. People live in the Arctic and are in touch by radio and TV. But in McClure's time, the Arctic was inaccessible. The explorers of the nineteenth century were cut off totally.

The Royal Navy sent ship after ship into the Arctic seeking the Passage. Ship after ship returned, often after its crew endured fearful hardships, with nothing to report. One such crew, under Sir John Ross, actually spent five years cut off from civilization. Given up for lost, Ross returned at last in the summer of 1833, having wrecked one of his two vessels. But he had not found what he had been seeking.

In 1845 another expedition was launched to search for the Passage. Its leader was a rather ordinary, but very likeable seaman named John Franklin. In his sixtieth year, he was far too old to attempt such a feat, but the British Admiralty let him go anyway, because he wanted the prize so badly. (See *Jane Franklin's Obsession* in this series.)

Franklin and his 129 men vanished into the Arctic mists and were never seen alive again. His two stubby little vessels, *Erebus* and *Terror*, were never found, though not for lack of trying. It was maddening! Somewhere in that maze of bald islands and wriggling channels, there *must* be some clues to Franklin's fate. But for years not a single clue could be found.

And so the search for the Passage was joined by a parallel search for Franklin and his men. Now there were two prizes dangled before the ambitious young men seeking fame and fortune. All of England wanted both mysteries solved.

It is difficult today to understand the wave of emotion and despair that washed over Great Britain when, in 1848, it became obvious that Franklin and his men were lost and probably dead. Public prayers were said in sixty churches for the safety of the expedition. Fifty thousand well-wishers attended.

That year the Royal Navy launched an ambitious three-pronged attack that would see one overland party and four ships explore the maze of islands and channels from three directions – east, west, and south.

For eighteen months these expeditions were out of touch with the world, and when they returned they had no shred of news concerning the missing men – no clues, no messages, *nothing*. One expedition made a remarkable seven-hundred-mile (1,120 km) journey in small boats along the northern Alaska coast from the Bering Sea to the Mackenzie delta, and returned empty-handed – establishing beyond doubt that Franklin had not gone west to that great river. In November of 1849, the two other expeditions limped back to England to report failure. One of them was commanded by a famous Antarctic explorer, Sir James Ross (a nephew of John Ross). It arrived home with six of the company of sixty-four dead, another twelve sick, and the commander's own health broken.

A kind of Arctic fever swept England. Books about polar journeys, huge paintings showing Arctic scenes, newspaper and magazine articles about northern adventure, all combined to stimulate the public to a fever pitch.

The British Navy decided to enlarge the search. Because James Ross had been blocked in Barrow Strait – in the eastern Arctic – by impassible ice conditions, the Navy, in the fall of 1849, turned its attention to the west. If ships couldn't pierce the unknown Arctic core from the east, perhaps they could enter the Arctic Ocean from Bering Strait in the west and proceed eastward.

Ross's two ships, *Enterprise* and *Investigator*, were available. An expedition was quickly outfitted. Captain Richard Collinson in the *Enterprise* would be its leader, and Lieutenant Robert McClure, who had been with Ross on the previous expedition, would be second-in-command, and in charge of the *Investigator*.

The two ships left Plymouth on January 20. This was only the first of six expeditions that would set off that year to search for John Franklin.

None of these searches was successful. But this great sweep of the mysterious Arctic, which continued for years, was not without its side benefits. Franklin had been sent to search for the fabled North West Passage. The searchers did not find Franklin himself, but they found the Passage and explored the maze of Arctic islands. And the man who got the credit was Collinson's second-in-command, Lieutenant Robert McClure.

The story of McClure and his voyage is the story of a man prepared to risk the lives of himself and his crew in order to achieve his ambition. But it is also the story of the opening up of a channel from west to east in the great maze

Robert McClure with Johann August Miertsching.

CHAPTER ONE

~

The Explorer and the Missionary

L ET US JOIN ROBERT MCCLURE as he strides the foredeck of the *Investigator* – a handsome man with a hawk's nose, an unruly shock of black hair, and a fringe of chin whiskers joined to his long sideburns.

On the horizon he can spot his sister ship, the *Enterprise*, under his superior, Richard Collinson. The Royal Navy never sends a single ship on such an expedition. Its vessels are to travel in pairs so that, in the event of disaster – and there have been many disasters – one ship can go to the aid of the other, and, if necessary, take her crew aboard.

Later events suggest that McClure was not entirely happy with this arrangement. He had two goals in mind, either of which would set him up for life. He would find Franklin and, in finding Franklin, he would also find the fabled Passage. He was not one to share this triumph with a fellow officer, especially one like the peppery Collinson, who outranked him. He wanted all the glory for himself.

He faced a long and difficult voyage. It would take his

ship from the British Isles to the tip of South America, around Cape Horn, and then across the Pacific to the Sandwich Islands (which we call Hawaii). The two ships would then sail north and west in a great circle around the long finger of the Aleutian Island chain that reaches almost to Asia. Having skirted the Aleutians, they would then head northeast again to the northern coast of Alaska, which belonged to Russia in the mid-1800s.

That journey would add up to more than 25,000 miles (40,000 km) – a distance equal to the circumference of the earth. When he reached Point Barrow on Alaska's Arctic coast, McClure would, at last, be at the entrance to the western Arctic. At the same time, far to the east, other ships, British and American, would also be searching for Franklin. The frozen world had never known such activity.

McClure is a fascinating character. He had spent twenty-six years in the Navy, but this was his first command and he intended to make the most of it. He knew that if he could either find Franklin or discover the Passage he would be the most famous man in England, as well as the richest naval officer of his day. Although most Arctic explorers were ambitious, McClure's ambition was more naked and less admirable. There is little doubt that McClure was out for McClure first, and everybody else second.

Although he made important discoveries, he was not generous enough to share his triumphs with others. Yet we must admire his daring. He took big chances and he won, even though he put his crew and himself in danger. And, like most successful explorers, he had his share of luck and knew how to make the most of it.

But it is also clear that McClure was unstable. He suffered spasms of uncontrollable fury when the progress of his expedition – and thus his own ambitions – was threatened.

He had waited a long time for this command. He came from an Army, not a Navy background. He was educated at the best places, Eton and Sandhurst, and joined the Navy quite late for a young Englishman – at the age of seventeen. (Many a young midshipman joined at the age of thirteen.) He had served on two previous Arctic expeditions. The first, in 1836, was disastrous. The second, in 1848, when he was a lieutenant under James Clark Ross, gave him more experience.

He was not comfortable in command. He kept to himself and was not an easy man to know. He didn't care much for his own officers, who were young, inexperienced, and often slovenly. Many, in fact, were incompetent. And his crew was unruly and often sullen.

McClure really didn't know how to deal with them as many other commanders did. He flogged his men unmercifully for minor breaches of discipline. His cook, for instance, was given forty-eight lashes for swearing. Yet, though he often put his own fierce ambitions ahead of his crew's safety, in moments of real danger he had the ability to gather his men together and rally them with a few words.

Unlike his predecessor, Edward Parry (see *Parry of the*

Arctic in this series), he made no attempt to lessen the boredom of an Arctic winter. Parry had brought along a magic lantern, arranged for theatrical performances, and even published a newspaper to keep his crew mentally healthy. McClure's men were left largely to their own devices.

Still, he managed to survive through four winters – from 1850 to 1854 – with very little of the discord that marked so many other Arctic voyages. He did this partly through tough discipline, but also because in a tight spot he was able to rouse his men to superhuman effort.

It wasn't in Robert McClure's makeup to be on friendly terms with his officers. His closest companion, oddly enough, was a civilian, Johann August Miertsching. Miertsching was a Moravian missionary from Labrador who had been brought along because he spoke the native tongue and could act as an interpreter. Perhaps because he was a civilian, McClure felt Miertsching could in some way relax the formality that he thought proper to his command.

Miertsching, a pious young evangelist, was thirty-two years old and a favourite of everybody. Strong, cheerful, never in a bad temper, he had been long accustomed to the conditions of Labrador, which were similar to those of the Arctic. And unlike the British sailors who dressed in their wool uniforms, he wore Inuit clothing. He also got along well with McClure. The fairest descriptions we have of the expedition come from his own accounts.

Following their departure from Plymouth, the *Enterprise* and the *Investigator* sailed down the east coast of North and South America to the Straits of Magellan at the very tip. The fog was so thick it was obvious they couldn't stay together, so Collinson arranged with McClure to meet off Cape Lisburne, on the west coast of Alaska.

Now McClure was on his own. His first port of call would be Honolulu in the Hawaiian Islands. But the voyage wasn't happy. Miertsching especially, who had no experience of life aboard a British warship, was shocked by the crew, whom he thought insolent and Godless. "I feel as if my lot had been cast among half a hundred devils," he wrote. "The harsh rules of naval discipline are barely enough to keep them under control."

This was the year of the California Gold Rush. Ships loaded with adventurers were racing for the west coast. The *Investigator*, having rounded Cape Horn, was on a different tack, heading directly for Hawaii through weather so dreadful that seventeen of the crew were sick.

Then, on May 15, the ship was almost lost. McClure's first officer, William Haswell, had left the deck for a few minutes, and in that brief time a squall struck the ship a dreadful blow, smashing all three masts.

McClure flew into a fury – "the most unpleasant that I have yet experienced," according to Miertsching. The captain put his first officer under arrest for his neglect. After that his anger subsided as quickly as it had arisen.

Later, McClure seemed to regret this moment of ungovernable fury, which Miertsching described as "positively inhuman." When the missionary fell ill, McClure took him into his cabin and poured out his apologies. He seemed to regret "that he had forgotten himself and had not handled the affair as a sincere Christian should have done."

But McClure himself was not particularly religious. "At sea," he told the missionary, "a man must have experience and not hang his head." He told Miertsching he was not yet a true seaman, and described a naval officer he once knew who had tried to practise "land Christianity" aboard a man-of-war. "He learned by experience that it did not serve on board a ship; so he gave up the sea, and became a parson and wrote tracts for old wives."

McClure scoffed at the missionary's practice of handing out religious tracts to the crew. He'd do better, he said, to give them to "loose women," who would receive them with more thanks than the sailors did. But the day would come when the Arctic would shake McClure out of his cynicism, as it shook so many others.

CHAPTER TWO

~

A daring gamble

THE *Investigator* REACHED Honolulu harbour on July 1, 1850. Now, to his alarm, McClure learned that Collinson, his superior, had lingered four days and then decided to wait no longer. He had set sail the previous morning for Bering Strait, which separates Alaska and Siberia. This hasty departure, as we shall see, doomed Collinson to a minor position in the list of Arctic heroes.

Collinson had left word that if McClure didn't catch up he would head east at once into the maze of the Arctic islands. The British supply ship *Plover*, which had been anchored in the strait since 1849, would go with him.

That was too much for McClure. Was he to be denied his chance at fame and fortune? He was in a frenzy to get moving. He had planned to get rid of some of his officers, especially Haswell who was still under arrest. But now every hour counted. He allowed Haswell to make a suitable apology and signed him on again.

In a perfect whirlwind of activity, he worked around the

clock to get his ship loaded with provisions and to round up his crew members. Many had celebrated so well that they were now in jail in Honolulu. He paid their fines, but found they were not fit for duty. It must have been a colossal bender! Two weeks later, several were still on the sick list, not yet recovered from what Miertsching called "the frightful excesses in Honolulu."

McClure managed to get his men rounded up and his ship into shape in just three days. At six o'clock, on the evening of July 4, he left the tropical Hawaiian waters behind and headed north to the Arctic. He had decided upon a daring, but dangerous gamble. He wouldn't just catch up with Collinson. He would beat him to Cape Lisburne on the northwest tip of Alaska! Then he would try to get ahead of him, in what was now turning out to be a race for the western Arctic.

The expedition had been ordered to circle around the outer islands of the Aleutian chain. That would take them close to the Kamchatka Peninsula of Asia. That was the way Collinson had gone. This long, 1,100-mile (1,800 km) finger of volcanic islands was a mystery. No one had charted it. Masked by a thick cloak of fog, the Aleutians were subject to violent tides, which swept over shoals and reefs that could cause an unwary captain to wreck his ship. McClure decided on a bold and dangerous gamble: he would take a huge shortcut through this dangerous island chain, cutting through them at the eastern end.

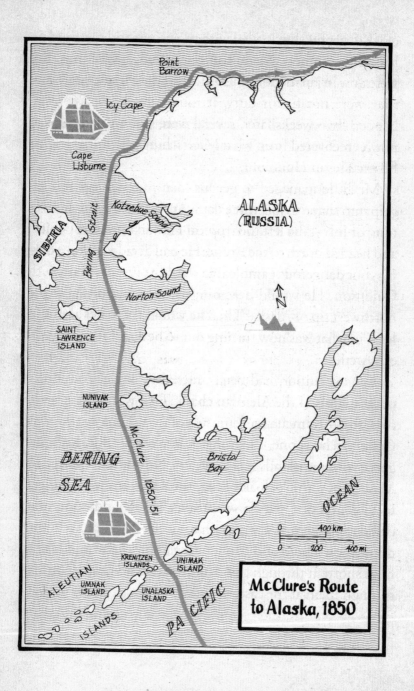

Point
Barrow

Icy Cape

Cape
Lisburne

Kotzebue Sound

ALASKA
(RUSSIA)

SIBERIA

Bering Strait

Norton Sound

N

SAINT
LAWRENCE
ISLAND

NUNIVAK
ISLAND

McClure 1850-51

BERING

SEA

Bristol
Bay

OCEAN

0   400 km
200   400 mi

ALEUTIAN

UMNAK
ISLAND

KRENITZEN
ISLANDS

UNALASKA
ISLAND

UNIMAK
ISLAND

ISLANDS

PACIFIC

**McClure's Route
to Alaska, 1850**

The gamble succeeded. McClure reached Kotzebue Sound just south of Cape Lisburne on July 29. The journey had taken just twenty-five days – half the time it would have taken to sail around the Aleutians.

Kotzebue Sound lies at the northern limits of Bering Strait, and there McClure spied the British depot ship, *Plover*. There was no sign, of course, of Collinson who was taking the long route. McClure sailed on to the rendezvous point at Cape Lisburne. On the way he was hailed by another Royal Navy vessel, the frigate *Herald*, commanded by Captain Henry Kellett, whose job it was to keep the *Plover* supplied with provisions.

At this point McClure engaged in a bald deception – which did not fool Kellett, an experienced commander. McClure pretended to believe that Collinson had gone on *ahead* of him. That, of course, was impossible. Kellett knew how long it would take to get around the Aleutian Islands. Collinson, he reckoned, must be at least twenty days behind McClure.

Yet here was McClure proposing to enter the dangerous Arctic without any escort vessel. The orders had been quite clear: the two ships were supposed to stick together. McClure ignored those instructions. He pretended he was actually trying to follow the Navy's instruction by catching up with his superior!

Kellett, who outranked him, could have stopped him. In fact he tried. But he was reluctant to give a direct order. McClure kept up the pretence – even kept some personal mail for Collinson, which he said he would deliver when they met. But of course they never did meet.

Kellett tried to get him to wait at least forty-eight hours. McClure refused. In fact, he all but dared the senior officer to stop him – and that Kellett wouldn't do. The British Navy had not figured on this. There were no instructions as to what should be done if the ships failed to meet off the Alaska coast. And so Kellett let McClure go.

Away he went into the grinding confusion of the ice pack. A tongue of ice, solid as granite, blocked his way. With a wind behind him, McClure ordered up every shred of canvas, then boldly turned his prow into the very centre of the mass. The *Investigator* shuddered and almost came to a stop. The masts trembled so violently they seemed about to shake the ship to pieces. Then the ice split under the force of the blow, and they were through into open water. McClure had won the second of his gambles.

Now, with the wind against her, the *Investigator* would have to be towed around Point Barrow at the northwest tip of Alaska. That took forty men in five boats, pulling on the oars until they were exhausted. That task completed, they entered unknown waters. Ninety miles (144 km) to the north, the captain could see the permanent polar ice pack – a stupendous, glittering wall of white, centuries old. He had never seen anything like that before in the eastern Arctic.

His ship groped her way along the northern coast of

Alaska, often moving up blind channels and returning to the main one, sometimes trapped in the ice for hours, even days. At last McClure passed the great Mackenzie delta. He was seeking Banks Island, which Parry, the first of the Arctic explorers, had spotted in the distance years before.

This was unknown country. Many of the natives whom they met had never seen a white man. McClure and his officers worried about their souls and their lack of civilization, for they believed that every native should become a Christian.

Now the man who had dismissed the idea of Christianity, in his talk with the Labrador missionary, wrote that he hoped "some practically Christian body … could send a few of their brethren amongst the tribes … to carry to them the arts and advantages of civilized life, and trust in God, in his own good time, showing them the way to eternal life." It did not occur to McClure, or indeed to any other officer of the Royal Navy, that there were many forms of life, civilized and otherwise, which were just as cultured and accomplished as those McClure knew.

The attitude to the Inuit, who in those days were known as Eskimos, was at best patronizing, and at worst racist. The ship's doctor, Alexander Armstrong, thought them "the most filthy race on the face of the globe … thieving, cunning … treacherous and deceitful.…" He trusted that "the day is not far distant when the light of civilization will dawn on this poor, benighted but intelligent race of human

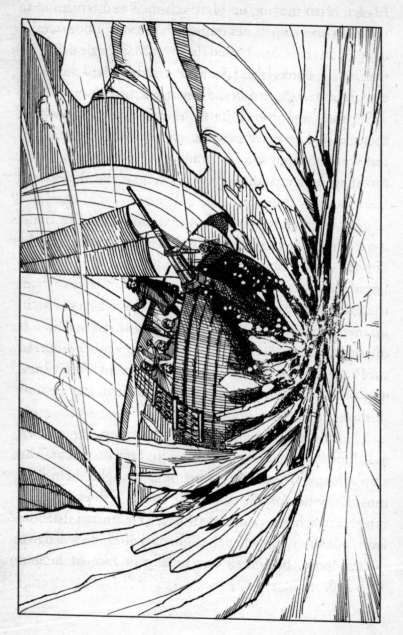

The Investigator plunges through the ice.

beings." He thought that the Hudson's Bay Company had made no effort to remove them from what he called "a state of heathen darkness."

The natives were equally bewildered by the white men. They thought the ship had been carved out a single, enormous tree, and wanted to know where such trees grew. Community property was part of their way of life, and so they thought nothing of taking any object they wanted. One enterprising man even went so far as to slip his hand into McClure's pocket, while a woman tried to conceal a large anvil by hiding it under her, like a hen sitting on an egg. This misunderstanding of their views confirmed the British in their belief that the Inuit were an immoral lot, desperately in need of divine guidance.

At Cape Bathurst, northeast of the Mackenzie delta, the Inuit were enchanted by Miertsching, who spoke their language, wore clothes like theirs, and told them wonderful and exciting tales about a great good spirit who had created the sun, moon, stars, rocks, and water. They accepted it all with amazement and wonder. They had their own concept of heaven and hell, remarkably like the Christian one – a good land with a good spirit who looked after animals so they didn't disappear from the land, and a bad land with a bad spirit who did great harm. They believed that each person who died would be sent to the destination he had earned in life.

Miertsching was beginning to love these simple, cheerful people. He didn't want to leave them. In fact, their chief pleaded with him to stay and tell him more of his marvellous stories, even offering his sixteen-year-old daughter as his bride. A throng followed him to the beach where fifteen kayaks paddled off to the ship to bid him farewell. But Miertsching, too, worried about their souls.

Miertsching could not stay, much as he might have wanted to. The ice was already gathering along the shore. Winter was settling in. Ahead lay the unknown, and somewhere hidden in that glittering, frozen mass lay Franklin's missing ships. Was it too much to hope that somewhere, too, in that maze of friendless islands, was to be found the elusive Passage?

CHAPTER THREE

~

The Passage at last

THE *Investigator* SLOWLY SAILED EAST between the gathering masses of ice. The land on the right began to rise until, on the western side of Franklin Bay, the cliffs soared to seven hundred feet (213 m). McClure tried to keep going, but the ice blocked his way. He was forced north in a zigzag course towards a lofty, mountainous land of dizzy cliffs, backed by two-thousand-foot (610 m) peaks.

There, on August 7, under a towering mass of rock that he named Lord Nelson Head (after the famous British admiral who was killed in 1805), McClure planted a flag and took possession of the territory. He named it Baring Land, after the first lord of the British Admiralty. He didn't know yet that he had actually landed on Banks Island, which he had been trying to reach ever since leaving Point Barrow.

Luck was on his side. He was imprisoned by the moving ice and couldn't even move around the southern shore of the new land. The ice was totally in charge, driving him steadily northward, up a narrow channel that followed the eastern shore of the island. He had no idea as to whether this was a dead end or not. If it was a strait, it might indeed be part of the North West Passage.

On September 9, he was just sixty miles (96 km) from the western end of Barrow Strait. That meant he was only sixty miles from territory that had already been explored. Here was the final gap to connect the east and the west.

McClure could not contain his excitement. "I cannot describe my anxious feelings," he wrote. "Can it be possible that this water communicates with Barrow's Strait, and shall be the long sought North west Passage? Can it be that so humble a creature as I am will be permitted to perform what has baffled the talented and wise for hundreds of years!" He praised God for having brought him so far without mishap. But he didn't mention the main object of his search. John Franklin's name does not occur at this point in his journal.

But he could go no farther. On September 17, young ice forming in front of him made it impossible to continue. He had come as far as he could that season. Now he had a decision to make. Should he try to find an anchorage farther south in some sheltered bay? Or should he allow his ship to become frozen in?

A lookout in the crow's nest – nothing more than a barrel attached to the top of the mast – could see twenty miles (32 km) to the north. In the distance the land tapered off to the northeast and the northwest leaving a clear expanse of water beyond. Now McClure knew he was on the edge of a great discovery. For Barrow Strait lay ahead, and beyond that, Melville Island. That had been explored by Sir Edward Parry thirty years before. In short, the last link in the North West Passage was in sight.

McClure was determined to stay in the pack ice. He knew it was dangerous, but he hadn't come this far to turn back. He had no intention of giving up the ground he had gained.

He had expected to be trapped in the ice, but instead he was caught in the moving pack. A dreadful gale, blowing down the channel, forced the ice south, and with it his ship, which was anchored to a vast floe. Like an unhorsed rider in a cattle stampede, McClure was helpless.

The *Investigator* was carried directly back the way she had come. For more than a week, she was in daily peril. She was swept thirty miles (48 km) south, then whirled about and forced north again. Now she was in danger of being crushed against the cliffs of the newly discovered Princess Royal Islands in the middle of Prince of Wales Strait.

On September 26, McClure was prepared to abandon ship. He ordered a year's provisions stacked on the deck ready to be thrown into the boats if the ship went down. The men stood by with bundles of warm clothes, their pockets stuffed with ammunition for hunting, and biscuits to eat. If necessary they were prepared to leap from the ship and try to struggle to the shore across the grinding ice.

The following night was even worse. They kept a seventeen-hour vigil, and during that time huge bergs, some of them three times as big as the ship, crashed against its sides until the oakum that was used for caulking squeezed from the seams.

Convinced they were doomed, the seamen abandoned all discipline. They broke open casks of liquor on deck and became roaring drunk. As the ship was flung over on her side, an enormous heap of crushed ice threatened to bury her and all the sixty-six men aboard. Then, miraculously, the gale died and the ship righted herself.

What had happened to save them? The explanation was simple enough. It was so cold that the rampaging ice had been frozen into a solid, unmoving sheet. Exhausted and limp, shocked into silence, the drenched and drunken sailors tried to grab some rest. The pressure had been so great that ropes nine inches (23 cm) thick had been snapped like threads, tearing all six ice anchors away.

With the storm over and two feet (61 cm) of water pumped out of the hold, McClure, who had scarcely spoken a word since the turmoil, mustered his crew and coldly read out the Articles of War regarding ship's discipline. He followed this with a savage tongue-lashing in which he called them a band of thieves, unworthy of the name of Englishmen. He was ashamed, he said, that such a rabble should walk the decks of a British ship. He promised that those who had opened the casks of liquor would be punished. Then he relented and reminded his men of the miracle that had saved them. Human strength had been ineffective; almighty Providence had preserved them from certain death. His words brought tears to the eyes of the most hardened seamen, who cheered their captain and promised to mend their ways.

The terrible trial that all had gone through had sobered both the men and the officers. McClure was now the commander of a happier ship. He himself took to reading the Bible, morning and night. As Miertsching put it, "he seems now to realize that he is not the good exemplary Christian which he used to think himself."

It was now October, 1850. At this point, some five hundred miles (800 km) to the northeast, eight British ships lay frozen into the ice of Barrow Strait. In addition, two American vessels had been trapped in the moving ice pack in Wellington Channel. Of course, McClure had no way of knowing that. With his own ship sealed, covered, and protected by a vast wall of ice, he turned his attention again to the North West Passage.

McClure had to be absolutely sure that the water the lookout in the crow's nest had seen in the distance really was a continuation of Barrow Strait. And so, on October 10, he took a sledge party across the ice to the land on the east side of the frozen channel. He named it Prince Albert Land, after Queen Victoria's husband. Actually it was a peninsula of the vast Victoria Island.

Accompanied by Dr. Armstrong and a few companions, McClure struggled up a fifteen-hundred-foot (457 m) mountain, panting from the unaccustomed exercise. From that vantage point, he saw in the distance the end of the

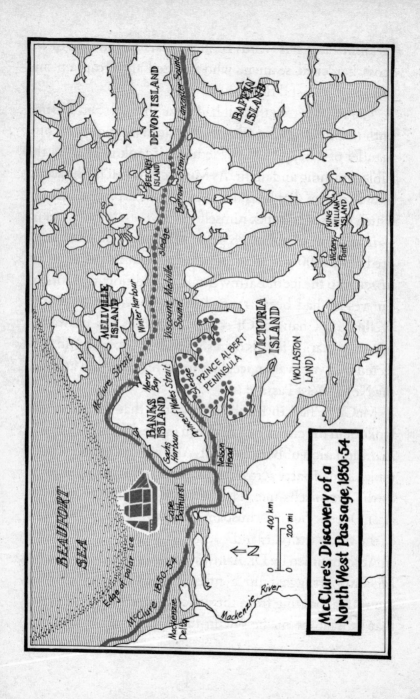

McClure's Discovery of a North West Passage, 1850-54

BEAUFORT SEA

Edge of Polar Ice

McClure 1850-54

Mackenzie Delta

Mackenzie River

Cape Bathurst

Nelson Head

Sachs Harbour

BANKS ISLAND

Mercy Bay

Prince of Wales Strait

Sledge

PRINCE ALBERT PENINSULA

McClure Strait

Winter Harbour

MELVILLE ISLAND

Sledge

Viscount Melville Sound

VICTORIA ISLAND

(WOLLASTON LAND)

Victory Point

KING WILLIAM ISLAND

Barrow Strait

Beechey Island

Lancaster Sound

DEVON ISLAND

BAFFIN ISLAND

N

0   400 km
0   200 mi

ice-packed channel that he had named Prince of Wales Strait. The doctor was convinced that "the highway to England from ocean to ocean lay before us." That wasn't good enough for McClure. He himself would have to set foot on the shore of the Passage.

Eleven days later he led another sledge party on a second exhausting journey along the eastern shore of Banks Island to the end of the channel. And there, five days later – October 26, 1850, a fine, cloudless day – Robert McClure, standing on a six-hundred-foot (183 m) neck of land, finally confirmed that he had reached the water route from Atlantic to Pacific.

"Thank God!" one of his crewmen muttered, as the sunrise brightened to reveal the land ahead curving off to the north toward a strait that would be named for McClure and to the southeast toward Melville Sound. Obviously the Passage was useless. Prince of Wales Strait was blocked, and no ship was ever likely to force its way through the ice stream by this route. That didn't matter to McClure. Nor did it matter that though he had seen the Passage from afar, he hadn't conquered it. He knew now his name would go down in the history books as the man who had made the greatest sea-going discovery of the age.

It was just as well he did not know then that some of John Franklin's men had found another North West Passage two years earlier. In the years that followed, the public would favour the more popular explorer. But nobody could take away from Robert McClure this moment of triumph.

Dr. Armstrong confessed to "an indescribable feeling of pride and pleasure" at the thought that "the maritime greatness and glory of our country were still further elevated above all nations of the earth; the solution of this great enigma leaving nothing undone to confirm Great Britain's Queen – Empress of the Sea...."

That was laying it on pretty thick. Even the Inuit didn't bother to go that far north. What the search for the elusive Passage had accomplished was to so concentrate the British

Triumph! McClure finds a North West Passage.

on northern exploration that by the end of the century the entire Arctic would be mapped and the waters charted.

McClure got back to his ship October 31. He was thin and exhausted, having rushed on ahead of his crew, lost his way, and wandered about without sleep for an entire Arctic night. He was taken on board unable to speak, his limbs stiff with cold, looking more like a corpse than a living human being.

Two days later he formally told his crew about his

discovery. They would share in the reward that had been offered for finding the Passage. He told them he hoped they would be home with their families within a year. For that they gave him three hearty cheers, three more for the Queen, three for the discovery, three more for the rest of the officers, and three for their sweethearts and wives. They followed that with one final cheer, and everybody got grog and extra meat for supper.

In victory, McClure was unusually humble. "The world may speak of me or the ship as having done this but a higher power than me has directed us," he said. The sledge journey had exhausted him and for the next month he was confined to his cot.

CHAPTER FOUR

~

Mercy Bay

MCCLURE HADN'T QUITE FORGOTTEN that the main object of the expedition was to search for John Franklin. He sent out three sledge journeys the following spring. With these he also hoped to solve several geographical puzzles. He wanted to know which lands he had discovered were attached to the land mass of North America and which were islands.

The sledgers didn't get away until April, 1851. They were not enthusiastic about these journeys. The harbour was not sheltered, and the *Investigator* was in a dangerous position in the very middle of Prince of Wales Strait, which was still frozen. Most of the men who left thought themselves doomed. They didn't expect to find the ship in one piece when they got back.

McClure knew that there would be a terrible upheaval when the ice broke. He had already placed a depot on one of the Princess Royal Islands with three months' provisions in case the ship should be crushed by the rampaging ice. If that happened, he hoped they might be able to travel toward the Mackenzie delta by small boat or sledge, and then go up that river to the nearest trading post. But that was a long shot at best.

With the threat of shipwreck hanging over them, the tensions among the crew and officers returned. One sledge party was told to follow the south shore of Melville Sound toward Cape Walker. Unfortunately, its captain, Robert Wynniatt, broke his chronometer (a naval timepiece) a week after he left. He used this as an excuse to hurry back to the ship. McClure thought he had come back with news of Franklin and flew into a rage when he learned the real reason. He sent Wynniatt back immediately without a new chronometer – an absurd and senseless act.

Lieutenant Samuel Cresswell's party, which was sent to explore the northeast coast of Banks Island, also came back a week early. Two men were suffering from frostbite, and another had to have part of his foot amputated. Those who weren't disabled were sent out again after only two days' rest to chart the south shore of Banks Island. That was another harsh decision by McClure.

He was bitterly disappointed that none of the parties had managed either to find Franklin or to fulfil their other assignments. In fact, he would have been even angrier had he known that Wynniatt's party at one point was just a few miles from one of the sledges from a ship sent out to search for Franklin from the east.

There was one journey that McClure could have made that he neglected – it was a failure that would cause untold hardships. Only a hundred miles (160 km) to the north was Sir Edward Parry's old winter camp on Melville Island. Parry had left a cairn there, and it was more than likely that the searchers from the other end of the Arctic would visit it. If McClure had left a message at Parry's cairn, they would know where he was. In truth, one party did visit the cairn, seeking just such a message, and found nothing. McClure's neglect doomed him to spend three more winters in the Arctic.

The three sledge journeys turned up nothing. McClure tried again. A hundred miles south, on the shores of Prince Albert Land, the party under Lieutenant Haswell had discovered a new band of Inuit. McClure had decided now to seek these people out in hopes that they could tell him something about the lost Franklin expedition.

Off he went at a cracking pace, taking six men and Miertsching, the missionary. There, on June 2, he reached the tents of the natives, and there, to his astonishment, an Inuit woman drew an almost perfect chart of the area on the paper he supplied. It showed the entire coastline of North America, which none of the natives had ever visited, and it filled up blanks on the existing maps. The Inuit, as other explorers had already learned, were expert map-makers.

The Inuit were astonished to learn that there were other lands inhabited by human beings. McClure found them both friendly and intelligent. Their simple habits brought out in him an unexpected tenderness, and when it came time to depart, Miertsching noted that "the captain was so grieved at leaving these loving people helpless in this frightful region of ice that he could not refrain from tears."

A touching little scene followed. In a sudden gesture, McClure took off his thick red shawl and wound it around the neck of a young woman who was standing nearby with a child on her back. She was startled. The idea of gift-giving was foreign to these people. It was part of their code always to offer something of equal value in return, but she had nothing to give him. And so she took the baby out from under her hood, covered it with kisses, and, in a remarkable gesture, offered it to McClure in exchange.

Miertsching had difficulty explaining that his captain wasn't proposing a trade. She understood at last and, laughing, accepted the shawl, which until then she had refused to touch. She wanted to know what animal it was that had a red skin. But there was no time to explain. One of the men was already suffering badly from frostbite, and McClure wanted to get back to the ship.

It is ironic that McClure, who showed a good deal of pity and concern for the Inuit, believed that, by Christianizing and "civilizing" them, he could better their condition. We know now that this attitude led only to a disruption of the native way of life, to infection by European diseases, and to the destruction of a value system that had worked perfectly well until the two peoples met each other. The exploration of the Arctic islands, hailed as a great achievement by the white European community, brought little but misery to the people whose lands were invaded.

McClure is offered a surprising gift.

Six weeks later, on July 14, the ice in Prince of Wales Strait broke up without incident. McClure headed back north hoping to skip through the North West Passage and complete the trip from Pacific to Atlantic. That, as it turned out, was not possible. The great ice stream that pours down from the north barred his way, as it had barred the way of other explorers.

On August 16, McClure made a sudden decision. He would sail south again and try to circle around Baring (or Banks) Land (in fact Banks Island). If it was an island, then he could get into the waters connected to Barrow Strait from the far side and still make his way through the famous Passage.

This was another daring, even foolhardy gamble. It was late in the year. McClure knew nothing of the fogbound, ice-choked channel he was planning to enter. He was chancing an encounter with what Miertsching correctly called "the frightful polar pack." He was risking his ship and the lives of his crew. He had discovered the Passage, he had searched vainly for Franklin, he could have gone back the way he had come. But McClure was a man obsessed. He had seen the Passage, but he had not sailed through it. He didn't want half the glory; he wanted it all.

He was astonished to find the channel to the south was free of ice. He sped down it in a single day, rounding Nelson Head with a fresh breeze spurring him on. By August 18 he had covered three hundred miles (480 km) without being held up by ice.

The white world came alive. Polar bears lumbered over the shore ice. Caribou pounded across the barren slopes. Seals basked in the sunshine. Geese, wild swans, and ducks rose in flocks from the water.

On the southwest corner of Banks Land, on what is now known as Sachs Harbour, he left a note in a cairn for his missing commander, Collinson, who found it three weeks later. But the two never met up with one another.

Meanwhile, McClure's luck continued to hold. He rounded the southwest cape of Banks Land and scudded north at speeds as high as seven knots (13 km/h). For a day he travelled up a broad lane of water created by the polar pack on his left and the island on his right. Then the lane began to narrow. The land rose. The pack drew closer, until it seemed they were in a kind of a canyon with high cliffs of ice on one side, rising a hundred feet (30 m) out of the sea, and the dizzier cliffs of rock towering above him on the other.

The *Investigator* was so close to the land that her boats had to be hauled up to prevent them from being smashed against the rock walls. By the time the ship stood off Cape Prince Alfred at the northwest corner of Banks Island, the channel wasn't any more than two hundred feet (60 m) wide. The crews had to take to the boats to tow the ship past the cliffs, blasting at them with black powder.

On August 20 the ship came to a halt with the ice pressing on her. Shore parties explored the headland and came upon an ancient forest – masses of petrified trees piled on hills and in gorges. Some of them had trunks ten inches (25 cm) thick, but now they had been turned to stone. Here was proof that this frozen land had once been a warm region with a thick forest and smiling meadows.

Now the Arctic returned to attack with all its fury. Again, the men were ordered on deck with their belongings, ready to leave at any instant. The high spring tide and the west wind hurled masses of ice down on the ship, again throwing her broadside against the floe to which she was anchored.

Beams cracked, doors sprang open. "This is the end!" McClure cried, "the ship is breaking up; in five minutes she will be sunk." He was about to cut the cables that attached them to the ice floe, when another miracle occurred. The ice suddenly became motionless.

By this time McClure was convinced a Higher Power was shielding him, that no lives would be lost, and that all would get back to their homes safely. His pale and trembling followers were clinging to the bulwarks, too shaken to speak. He got them together and promised he'd bring them to a safe harbour and would do his best to make life pleasant for them.

In fact, Robert McClure was a changed man. All the gambling spirit seemed to have been sucked out of him by this last encounter with the elements. Before many days had passed, the ship entered the main channel northeast of Banks Island that would later be named for McClure. Barrow Strait and Lancaster Sound, the continuation of the Passage, lay just ahead.

For most of September, the expedition moved to the southeast. The ship hugged the coast of Banks Island, a forbidding shore without a bay or a harbour that might offer shelter or protection; a journey, in Dr. Armstrong's words, that "should never be again attempted; and ... I feel convinced ... will never be made again."

But at last the *Investigator* reached a large bay. McClure named it Mercy Bay. Later the doctor remarked that some of the men thought it ought to have been called that because "it would have been a mercy had we never entered it." For the bay was a dead end. Here the crew would be confined for the next two years. The ship itself would never be able to leave.

Dr. Armstrong, who was always critical of McClure, thought that he should have gone on to Edward Parry's Winter Harbour, or even farther east to complete the transit of the Passage. It is more than possible he might have accomplished that feat. A few days later his sailing master found open water as far as the eye could see.

But McClure was taking no chances. What had happened to the daring captain who had once gambled on a fast shortcut through the Aleutians and a careless dash past the Arctic pack off Banks Island? Was it a failure of nerve as some would later say? Perhaps. But it must be remembered that he and his crew had come through a frightful experience. He had been lucky three times. And it was September 23, very late in the season.

For once, Robert McClure put the safety of his ship and

ship's company ahead of his personal ambitions. He could not know that this latest decision would come close to being the death of them all.

It was not an easy winter for Robert McClure and his men. In his haste to find a secluded harbour, he had chosen a trap – and he soon realized it. Suspecting that the ice in that sheltered backwater might not melt the following summer, he reduced rations. The doctor insisted the diet wasn't enough to keep the crew healthy. By April 1852, the men were losing weight at an alarming rate. But McClure stuck to his quota. When three half-starved men stole some meat, he had them flogged.

CHAPTER FIVE

The rescue

ONLY THREE SEARCH VESSELS remained in the Arctic that winter of 1851-52: McClure in the *Investigator* at Mercy Bay; Collinson in the *Enterprise*, anchored off Victoria Island on the eastern shore of Prince of Wales Strait; and, five hundred miles (800 km) to the east in Prince Regent Inlet (just west of Baffin Island), the little *Prince Albert*, hired by Lady Franklin. Everyone else had returned to England where press and public were demanding the Navy try once more to find Franklin and his men.

To this chorus was now added the voice of Lieutenant Cresswell's father, who was also demanding that there be a separate search for the *Investigator*, on which his son was serving. Nobody had heard a whisper of McClure and his ship since August, 1850.

In April, 1852, a five-ship squadron under an aging commander, Sir Edward Belcher, was ordered north to continue the search. That same month, McClure set off on a search of his own.

Travelling by sledge across the rough ice of the strait later named for him, he started for Parry's Winter Harbour on Melville Island – a journey that he should have made the previous year. And there, on the summit of a great sandstone block, he found a flat tin case containing a message for him. To his dismay he saw that it had been left there the previous June.

Now, as he realized the depth of his negligence and the seriousness of his position, Robert McClure sat down and wept like a child. The other ships searching for Franklin, he realized, must have gone home. By now his would-be rescuers were all back in England. Everything he had worked for, the triumphs he had achieved, the charting of new lands as well as the crowning discovery of them all – the Passage – were as dust. There was little hope of rescue; he would not live to bask in his success.

He got back to the ship in May. Scurvy was spreading through the crew. By July, sixteen men suffered from it. Dr. Armstrong was urging a better diet to help them regain their strength, but McClure, facing another winter in Mercy Bay, refused. Freshly killed musk-oxen and a quantity of wild sorrel helped to stall the disease. It was not enough, however, to stop the hunger. One desperate man stole a loaf of bread knowing that punishment awaited. He got three-dozen strokes of the cat-o'-nine-tails on his bare back.

McClure meant to stretch out his rations as long as he could. When August arrived it was clear that Mercy Bay would remain locked in the ice. It was shaped like a funnel –

fifteen miles (24 km) deep and seven miles (11 km) broad at the entrance, where shoals caught the ice to form a barrier. The previous September this opening had been free of ice. But this season of 1852 was a slow one. By August 27 the young ice was strong enough to allow the crews to skate to the shore.

Now once again the land turned white. The men had nothing to do. One, Mark Bradbury, was clearly going mad. Although McClure kept up a cheerful attitude, Miertsching could hear him praying and sighing alone in his cabin.

On September 9 he got his crew together and told them what they already suspected – they were stuck for another winter. He tried to cheer them up, promising that they would all get home safely. But then he was forced to reveal that the half rations they had been living on for the past year would be cut back again.

They were down to one meal a day. Most ate their ration of half a pound of salt meat raw because it shrank so much when it was cooked. A group got together and pleaded for more food. They said the men were so hungry they couldn't sleep. Again, McClure refused. And now another man, Sub-Lieutenant Robert Wynniatt, went mad from hunger. By the end of 1852, each man was thirty-five pounds (16 kg) lighter, and twenty were ill with scurvy.

As the winter dragged on, the health of the men grew worse. The two mental cases howled all night, contributing to the gloom. At one point Wynniatt tried to kill his

The desperate crew begs McClure for more food.

captain. Another sailor, stiff with the cold, fell and broke his leg. By the end of January, one clerk, Joseph Paine, and one of the mates, Herbert Sainsbury, were close to death.

The ship, too, seemed to be suffering. The bolts and fastenings cracked in the sixty-degree-below-Fahrenheit (−51°C) cold. Miertsching noted that the doctor's reports had reduced McClure to despair. "How it must affect our captain," he wrote, "... when he sees his once-strong, rugged and hearty crew wasted away and scarcely with the strength to hold themselves upright."

The captain had concocted a dangerous plan the previous fall, and now, on March 2, prepared to put it into operation. He had decided that twenty of the strongest men would stay with the ship. Those who could not last another winter would try to get to civilization. One party would head for the depot and boat he had cached at Princess Royal Island on Prince of Wales Strait. With the food from that depot, they might be able to reach the mouth of the Mackenzie River. Another would travel to Port Leopold on the northeast corner of Somerset Island, where James Clark Ross had left a boatload of supplies. They would try to reach the whaling grounds in Baffin Bay.

It was a reckless, desperate scheme. In effect, McClure was sending the sick men to their deaths. As the doctor knew, there wasn't any hope that in their weakened condition they could survive such a lengthy and difficult journey. Sixteen were hospitalized. The demented Wynniatt couldn't be made to understand that he was to leave the ship. Bradbury, in the doctor's words, "must be handled like an idiot child."

Even healthy men would find it difficult to make those long journeys. But McClure felt he had to take some action. If the forty weakest men stayed, they would surely die with the others. There was just a slim chance that the twenty-two who remained might get through – for one thing there would be fewer men to divide the food.

The strange thing is that those detailed to leave were delighted at the prospect, while those who were chosen to stay with the ship were bitterly disappointed. Apparently McClure didn't realize that if by some miracle the ship was saved and he got back to England with the survivors, he would never be able to raise his head again in civilized company for having abandoned the sick.

On April 5, just as the sledges were ready to go, John Boyle, one of the men designated to leave, died of scurvy. McClure called all hands to the quarterdeck and delivered another of those eloquent morale-building addresses that seemed to rally them. He told them to be true to themselves and to the service, not to despair, but to look forward to the future with determination. In the gloomiest hour, he said, relief might easily come.

The next day he and Haswell were walking on the ice with Miertsching discussing the problem of how to dig a grave for Boyle in ground that was frozen granite-solid.

"Sir," said McClure to the missionary, "if next year in Europe you neither see nor hear of me, then you may be sure that Captain McClure, along with his crew, has perished and lies unburied but wrapped in the fur coat which you gave me, enjoying a long and tranquil sleep until awakened on the Day of Resurrection by the Redeemer in Whom is all my hope and trust ..."

At that moment he was interrupted by one of his seamen, who rushed up to announce that something black was moving on the heavy ice near the sea. He thought it was a musk-ox, but it wasn't. A second seaman came running up.

"They are men," he cried. "First a man, then a sledge with men."

Apart from their shipmates, the seamen had not seen another human being for twenty-one months. Who were these? Inuit, perhaps? McClure and his companions held their breaths as one of the strangers drew nearer. He looked like a native with a face "as black as old Nick."

"In the name of God," cried McClure, "who are you?"

The stranger stepped forward and uttered a sentence that ran through them all like an electric shock. "I am Lieutenant Pim, late of the *Herald*, now of the *Resolute*...."

So the miracle that McClure had hoped for had come to pass. The relief he had promised his crew was at hand. Once again, in his darkest hour, Providence had smiled on Robert John Le Mesurier McClure.

CHAPTER SIX
A cruel decision

MCCLURE AND HIS MEN WERE saved because the British public, pushed on by the indomitable Lady Franklin, had refused to let the Royal Navy give up on the search.

In that spring of 1853, unknown to McClure, the five British naval vessels under the command of Sir Edward Belcher had taken up the task of finding the two lost expeditions. They were sent to look for Franklin, of course, but they were also looking for McClure and Collinson.

The previous September, one of the searchers, Leopold M'Clintock, had come upon McClure's letter written the previous April and left on the site of the Parry's Winter Harbour. The letter told of the *Investigator* being caught in the ice of Mercy Bay. It was too late in the season that year to rescue McClure. That would have to wait until the spring of 1853. But as early as possible – earlier than any spring journey yet made by the Navy in the Arctic – a small expedition set off on the rescue attempt.

At this point, McClure had been out of touch with the

outside world for two and a half years. He had no idea what was going on in the Arctic or elsewhere. His family had been unable to write him. The only letter he had dispatched had lain under the cairn at Parry's Winter Harbour for six months before it was discovered. Had Franklin been found? McClure had no way of knowing. Were there other vessels in the Arctic? Was anybody trying to find him? Like many Arctic explorers before him, McClure was totally in the dark.

The man who volunteered to find McClure was a remarkable young naval lieutenant, named Bedford Pim. He had been one of the last to see McClure before that expedition vanished into the western Arctic in the summer of 1850. Pim at that time was serving aboard the *Herald* under Captain Henry Kellett – the same Captain Kellett who had tried to stop McClure from making his rash dash into the heart of the Arctic maze. Now Kellett was in charge of two ships anchored off Melville Island. It was he who sent Pim on his voyage of relief.

Pim was not a typical naval man. He was an individualist who had earlier made an ambitious plan to cross Siberia in search of Franklin. He wanted help from the Russians, but they had no money, and so, when he learned that Kellett was going north again, he volunteered to join him. Now, in March of 1853, he was sledging west across the frozen expanse of Melville Sound on a rescue mission.

It was typical of Pim that he took a small party of ten men with him – with one sledge only, and one small dogsled. When the man-hauled sledge broke down, Pim sent all but two of his party back and, always the loner, mushed on with his dogs. The temperature stood at fifty degrees below Fahrenheit (−46°C). It was slow going. It took him twenty-eight days to reach the cliffs of Mercy Bay. He moved along the sullen coastline seeking a cairn, not knowing that McClure's ship was hidden from view by the hummocky ice. At last, one of his men pointed to a black spot on the bay. Pim got out his telescope, saw it was a ship, left his sled behind and pushed forward throwing his hat into the air, and screeching into the wind.

A wild scene followed. When McClure finally identified his rescuer as a man he had last seen near Bering Strait – his face black with the soot of his coal-oil lamp – the news that he sent back to his ship was at first treated as a joke. Then came a celebration. The sick sprang from their beds. The tradesmen laid down their tools. All those who could crawl poured out of the hatchway. Some couldn't trust their eyes and began to touch and paw their rescuers.

Pim was shocked by their experience and even more shocked to learn that their next meal consisted only of a tiny piece of bread and a cup of weak cocoa. He sent back to his sledge for a package of bacon. His own men were so affected that tears rolled down their cheeks.

The next morning McClure got his crew together to remind them that he had urged them to trust the mysterious workings of the Almighty. And thus was averted a second Arctic tragedy, one that would have matched that of

Bedford Pim rescues the Investigator.

John Franklin. But the miseries of the *Investigator* party were not yet ended, for now the nasty side of McClure's character showed itself.

Kellett's man, Pim, had saved McClure. Thus it followed that Kellett and his crew were eligible for at least part of the prize of ten thousand pounds that Parliament had voted for the discovery of the North West Passage. McClure wanted to keep it all – and all the glory too. To do that he had to keep up the pretence that his men were healthy enough to sail the ship out of the Arctic and home to England, not helped by Kellett or anybody else. And so, he rushed off immediately to try to persuade Kellett that he was perfectly able to keep going.

In order to make the scheme believable, he left two instructions, both cruel. The twenty-four members of the crew who were desperately ill would leave on April 15 by sledge and make their way to Kellett's two vessels off Melville Island. The remainder were to stay with the ship and continue on the *same rations* that had brought them to a state of near starvation. This callous order was designed to show that the expedition didn't need any help.

By the time the party of sick set off, three more of the ship's company were dead. It was a ghastly journey – half of the men were so miserable and lame they couldn't stand upright. Their stronger comrades had to tend to their needs by day and even put them to bed at night. It was the spectacle of this scarecrow party of shrunken creatures, tottering forward, hollow-eyed, staring blankly ahead, that convinced Kellett that McClure couldn't carry on as he claimed he could.

Kellett now suggested McClure abandon his ship. But once again the wily McClure insisted he must obey his orders. He said he couldn't abandon the *Investigator* on his own responsibility. Kellett thought he was being noble. In fact, McClure was looking forward to a time when he would be able to swear with a straight face before an inquiry that he had been quite prepared to go on without help – in short, that he, and he alone, was the conqueror of the Passage.

Kellett suggested a compromise. McClure would go back to the ship with Dr. Armstrong, and, if the men were fit and willing, he would carry on. Armstrong, of course, was one of his severest critics, so McClure suggested that one of Kellett's surgeons also accompany them. But when they reached the *Investigator* on May 19, McClure, to his surprise and dismay, found that only four men out of twenty would volunteer to go on. Both doctors agreed they shouldn't, and that was it. Kellett's order to abandon his ship was now in effect, and the *Investigator* was left to her fate.

Meanwhile, the search for John Franklin and his missing ships continued. Sledging parties under Leopold M'Clintock – who commanded Kellett's sister ship – fanned out to explore the western Arctic and search for Franklin in the unlikely event that he'd managed to get that far. Struggling in harness like so many beasts of burden, dragging back-breaking loads as heavy as 280 pounds (127 kg) a man, sometimes trudging knee-deep in slush, they performed superhuman feats at enormous personal cost.

Was it really necessary to send out big ten-man sledges loaded down with supplies when two or three dog drivers could cover the same ground? Nobody, apparently, bothered to consider that.

By the time the sledge crews got back, the surviving members of the *Investigator*'s company were lodged aboard Kellett's two vessels. It must have seemed to them that their troubles were over. For here there was plenty of game, including ten thousand pounds (4,500 kg) of musk-ox and caribou meat that had been taken that summer.

With no sign of Franklin in the western Arctic, Kellett's plan was to take his ships back to Beechey Island, which had become the headquarters of the British search expedition. He set off when the ice broke on August 18, to the great joy of the men of the *Investigator*. Two transport ships, accompanied by a steamer, *Phoenix*, were due to arrive from England with supplies and mail. Then they would return and the men would be homeward-bound at last! It seemed to be too good to be true – and it was.

They reckoned without the Arctic weather. Kellett's two ships had scarcely moved more than a hundred miles (160 km) to the east before the ice closed in again. Now, McClure's men, who had suffered through three dreadful Arctic winters, faced a fourth.

A few got away because McClure wanted to get the news

of his discovery to England. He had already sent Cresswell to Beechey Island by sledge with the demented Wynniatt. There they met the steamer, *Phoenix*, carrying letters and dispatches from home. Her steam power had allowed her to break through the ice pack and open up a passage for the transport ships that brought the new supplies for the depot. In spite of this, one of the transports, *Breadalbane*, was crushed in the ice and sank in fifteen minutes, though her crew was rescued. More than a century later, in 1981, Canadian divers found her in 340 feet (104 m) of water.

At the end of August, the *Phoenix* managed to nose through the ice pack and get to England with Cresswell and his news. The discovery of the North West Passage was "a triumph not for this age alone but for mankind," in the words of Lord Stanley, the secretary of state for the colonies. Cresswell was reunited with his father, to whom, as much as to anyone, he owed his life.

And so the news was out: McClure had been found and he, himself, had found the North West Passage, though he had not been able to navigate it. No one had yet made it all the way through from one ocean to another, and no one would until Roald Amundsen managed the feat in a long trip that started in 1903 and ended in 1906 – half a century after McClure's first discovery.

CHAPTER SEVEN

~

The high cost of dawdling

MCCLURE HAD BEEN FOUND. But where was Collinson, his superior officer? The two were supposed to have stuck together, but the rash and ambitious McClure had rushed on ahead and made his discovery, leaving Collinson far in the rear.

In fact, Collinson was doomed to spend five winters away from home, and to be out of touch with the civilized world for three years. He was more prudent than McClure. He took no gambles and so he was cheated of the ultimate prize.

He had one other problem: he could not speak the native language because his interpreter, Johann Miertsching, the Moravian missionary, was not with him. Miertsching was supposed to have transferred from McClure's ship to Collinson's in Honolulu in the summer of 1850. But, as we have seen, Collinson left before he arrived. The result was that, even if Collinson had encountered natives who had some clue to Franklin's fate, he would not have been able to talk to them.

Collinson's ship was not a happy one. Problems began when he cautiously took the longer route to Bering Strait. The winds weren't as bad in the Aleutians as he had been told – and as the more daring McClure discovered. But even before he reached the Bering Sea in mid-August, Collinson seemed frightened of wintering in the Arctic and was already talking of going back to Hong Kong.

He had made a serious error in sailing around the northern coast of Russian Alaska. He believed the coastal waters were so shallow that it would be dangerous to get within fifteen miles (24 km) of the mainland. As it turned out, he was wrong. There was plenty of depth nearer the shore.

The permanent Arctic ice pack fifteen miles from the coast posed a more serious threat. Collinson reached Point Barrow at the northwest tip of Alaska – but wouldn't go nearer than twenty-five miles (40 km) off shore. Then he turned back. He was convinced that an Open Polar Sea lay to the northwest. But there was no Open Polar Sea, despite the belief of many mariners. From that point on, there was only solid ice.

His ice master, Francis Skead, wrote that "this cursed *polar basin* ... is one of the phantoms which has led to our failure." If it hadn't held them back, they might have found an open channel along the coastline. "We now end the season to continue to seek for what no one but the Captain believes has any existence." They were eighteen days behind McClure.

The *Enterprise* returned the way it had come, and

rounded the northwest corner of Alaska, heading south. On August 30 at Point Hope, south of Cape Lisburne, Collinson found what he had missed on the northern journey – a note in a cairn from Kellett reporting that McClure was ahead of him. He was astounded and angry. If only he had found the message earlier! Then he would have certainly pressed on and caught up with McClure. Still, there was time to catch up – or so his officers believed.

"For God's sake, go back at once, it is not now too late," the surgeon, Robert Anderson, pleaded.

"No, no!" Collinson replied, "I must seek Kellett."

Kellett was farther south at Grantley Harbour at this time in his ship, *Herald*. So was Thomas Moore in the supply ship *Plover*. Collinson reached them on September 1. According to Skead, Moore told him there was a good anchorage in a harbour off Point Barrow, and Kellett urged him to retrace his steps.

"If you make haste, Coll, you'll be able to winter at Point Barrow."

"No, no," said Collinson. "I'm not going to take *my* ship there."

Instead he dawdled, deciding to seek winter quarters somewhere on the northwest coast of Alaska. Two weeks dragged by before he decided to go north again. He got as far as Icy Cape on September 22, but finding no suitable harbour, he stopped. One of his officers offered to go on to Point Barrow alone to check the harbour there. Collinson refused, turned south again, and spent the winter at Hong Kong.

This was a costly decision. When he got back the following July, and once again rounded the Alaskan peninsula, it became painfully clear that, had he kept on and wintered at Point Barrow, he would almost certainly have caught up with McClure. Then the two of them would have shared the honour of discovering a North West Passage.

Now Collinson got himself trapped in the ice pack off Point Barrow. It turned out there was a lane of open water and none of the shoals he had feared. He tried to make for that open lane, but was helplessly pushed back westward. By this time his ice master, Skead, whom he had ignored, was scarcely on speaking terms with him. Skead was impatient to move ahead, especially as the sea was calm by August 12. But instead of putting his men to work hauling the ship through the lanes in the melting ice, Collinson insisted on waiting for the wind to improve.

In that short season every mile counted. Yet there was no sense of urgency aboard the *Enterprise*. An ordinary yachtsman might have taken his craft east, Skead thought – "aye & his wife and daughters to boot." He had never seen men have it so easy aboard any ship on which he'd served. "As we make so little progress when there are so few obstacles to our advance, I am afraid to think of what we shall do if we meet with difficulty from ice. Poor Sir John! God help you – you'll get none from us."

Collinson finally reached the southern tip of Banks Island on August 26, 1851, and took possession of it in the name of the Queen. He couldn't know that McClure had been there the year before and already named it Nelson Head. The following day, at the Princess Royal Islands, they discovered that McClure had also been there – just six weeks before.

They sailed up Prince of Wales Strait – again not knowing that McClure had been ahead of them – and were stopped by the ice as McClure had been. Turning back, they rounded Banks Island from the east, and there, once again, found that McClure had been on the ground before them. In fact, at this moment he was only two weeks in the lead.

If Collinson had gone ahead, he could easily have wintered with the *Investigator* at Mercy Bay and taken charge of the combined expedition. But again he turned back, and on September 13 went into winter quarters on the eastern coast of Prince of Wales Strait at Walker Bay. This was then known as Prince Albert Land, but it is actually part of the massive Victoria Island, as Collinson himself was to discover. Once again, Collinson found that others had been there before him – the sledge crew of Lieutenant Haswell of the *Investigator*.

The weather remained fine. Five weeks went by before the ocean began to ice up. Collinson could have found a wintering harbour farther south and put himself in a better position for a thrust to the east the next spring. But he didn't.

His ice master was beside himself with frustration. "How much we have lost, it is painful to contemplate," he noted. His captain's inactivity was "a marvellous proceeding considering Franklin was perishing for food and shelter." Collinson's relations with Skead were so strained that by April, 1852, the ice master was put under permanent arrest.

The *Enterprise* left winter quarters that summer, and squeezed through Dolphin and Union Strait (south of Victoria Island) and through the island maze of Coronation Gulf – a remarkable feat of navigation on Collinson's part. But again, Collinson, without knowing it, was covering ground already explored by the men of the Hudson's Bay Company in the Franklin search.

The expedition wintered at Cambridge Bay on the southeastern shore of Victoria Island, no more than one hundred and twenty miles (192 km) from King William Island, which had not yet been explored. That, in fact, was where the clues to the loss of the Franklin expedition were to be found – for that is where the survivors had died.

Thus, Collinson could have solved the mystery of both the North West Passage and the fate of the lost explorer. Once again he muffed it. When he tried to question the natives who visited the ship that winter of 1852-53, he had nobody to translate. Almost certainly the Inuit had tales to tell of sinking ships and dying men only a few-score miles to the east. One of his officers, in fact, got some of the natives to draw a map of the coastline to the east. He thought the Inuit artists were indicating ships in that area. Collinson would have none of it.

In April 1853, Collinson led a sledging party up the west coast of Victoria Strait, and there he discovered a note in a cairn that told him that John Rae of the Hudson's Bay Company had covered the same ground two years before! Once again he had lost out on his discovery.

If he had only known earlier, he could have crossed Victoria Strait to King William Land and found the secret of the missing expedition. Victory Point, where the clues to the mystery lay hidden in a cairn of rocks, was less than forty miles (64 km) away. But Collinson, always cautious, worried about the roughness of the ice, and so the opportunity passed him by.

The frustrated Skead thought the whole area could and should have been investigated. "Two serving officers in good health & strong were under arrest on trifling charges," he wrote, adding that there were plenty of men available also to explore the estuary of the Great Fish River. But Collinson wasn't listening to Skead.

In July one of his crew members came upon some wreckage not far from Cambridge Bay. This included a fragment of a door frame that almost certainly came from one of

Franklin's ships. Collinson missed its significance. His fuel was running low, and so he turned west again to winter at Camden Bay on the north coast of Alaska.

When the *Enterprise* finally reached Port Clarence on the west coast of the Alaskan peninsula on August 24, 1854, the officers of the British supply ship *Rattlesnake* were shocked at the state of discipline that existed on board. At that point every one of Collinson's executive officers was under arrest. None had been allowed off the ship for fifteen months. Skead had been confined for two years and eight months.

When Collinson finally returned to England in May, 1855, he had managed to visit and explore all the mysterious "lands" that might or might not have been islands – Banks, Baring, Wollaston, and Victoria. He had sailed up Prince of Wales Strait, and had got as far as Victoria Strait directly across from King William Island, and yet his voyage was a failure because he discovered nothing new. Wherever he went he found others had gone before him.

Had he been a year or two earlier, he might have emerged as one of the greatest of the Arctic explorers. As it was, he returned to England with the reputation of a man who had simply covered old ground. His reception was chilly, not because of his failures, but because he was in trouble with his own officers. At one time or another they had all been under arrest. Now he demanded that they all be court-martialled, but the British Admiralty would have none of that. It was understandable that, after four years cooped up on a crowded ship, even disciplined men would feel the tension.

The embattled captain had only one claim to fame. He had shown that the narrow passage along the North American coastline could actually be navigated by a large ship. Until that point, it had not been believed possible. And that was the passage that Roald Amundsen eventually followed. In short, there was more than one North West Passage. There were in fact three.

Collinson emerged from his long Arctic confinement a bitter man. He was angry because the Navy refused to court-martial his officers. He was even more angry when the committee investigating claims to the discovery of the Passage passed him by.

Robert McClure and his crew got ten thousand pounds for their discovery. Collinson got nothing more than an honourable mention. Richard Collinson was so upset with the Admiralty that he never again applied for a naval command. Nor did anybody rush to offer him one.

As for Robert McClure, he, too, faced moments of anti-climax. In spite of the rewards and honour heaped upon him, there was still a suspicion that Franklin had discovered a North West Passage before McClure. And that later turned out to be true. In 1859 Leopold M'Clintock, working for Lady Franklin, discovered the relics of her husband's lost expedition on King William Island. As a result the missing explorer was credited with being the first to discover a North West Passage, making it clear that no single channel ran through the Arctic islands.

Whether or not Franklin had actually seen the Passage as it led through Victoria Strait in Queen Maud Gulf could never be known. But he had got close enough to it to make it likely, and sentiment was on his side, thanks to his widow's determined efforts to memorialize his name (see *Jane Franklin's Obsession* in this series).

And so this sentimental decision downgraded McClure's later discovery of another passage farther north. Unlike Franklin, McClure had actually traversed the Passage from east to west, though not entirely by water. But Franklin was a popular favourite. McClure's naked ambition had given him a brief moment of glory, but, in the end, it reduced him to the second rank of polar explorers. Nonetheless, he prospered. Knighted by the Queen, Sir Robert was posted to the China seas and ended his days as a vice-admiral.

The story of the search for the North West Passage is made up of tales – tales like McClure's – of disappointment, frustration, of naked ambition, and also of daring, courage, and resourcefulness. The rash Robert McClure and his more cautious commander, Collinson, are part of that story. Both their sagas are tied to the search for Franklin and the search for the North West Passage. But as in so many other cases, it was the search itself that counted, not the goal. Their real contribution was to open up the mysterious, frozen Arctic world – a world of treeless, wind-swept islands, some vast, some tiny, which we know now as the Arctic archipelago.

This archipelago is part of Canada today because of men like McClure, Collinson, Pim, and Kellett – and John Franklin himself.

INDEX

explorers of, 10-12, 13, 16, 17;
motives of for seeking Passage,
12;
and search for John Franklin, 14,
15, 19, 53, 60, 65-66;
and search for McClure and
Collinson, 53, 60-62, 63
Russia, 19, 61

SACHS HARBOUR, 49
Sainsbury, Herbert, 57
Sandwich Islands, *see* Hawaii
Scurvy, 7, 54, 58
Siberia, 24, 61
Skead, Francis, 69, 70, 71, 73, 74,
75
Somerset Island, 57
South America, 19
Stanley, Lord, 67
Straits of Magellan, 22

Terror, 13

UNION STRAIT, 73
United States, and search for
Franklin, 19

VICTORIA ISLAND, 37, 45, 53, 72,
73, 75
Victoria, Queen, 9, 37
Victoria Strait, 74, 75, 77
Victory Point, 74

WALKER BAY, 72
Wellington Channel, 37
Winter Harbour, 51, 54, 60, 61
Wollaston Island, 75
Wynniat, Sub-Lieutenant Robert,
44, 55, 57, 67

Coming Soon

BEFORE THE GOLD RUSH

Before news of the great Klondike gold strike was heard around the world, several hundred fortune-seekers were already scrabbling for gold along creek banks in the Yukon and Alaska.

Cut off from the world, clustered in squalid log towns with no link to civilization except a small steamerboat that arrived once a year with provisions, these free-spirited individuals made their own laws, with the power to execute or banish anyone who broke them. Many were strange characters, men with names like Cutthroat Johnson and Jimmy the Pirate. And when gold was found on the Klondike, most became millionaires – if only for a few months.

Before the Gold Rush is another instalment in Pierre Berton's vivid history of the Klondike Gold Rush of the late 1890s.